Conte

Introduction

As producer of the national television series *Off the Vine* I have travelled around Australia meeting our nation's best winemakers and sampling their superb wines. It hasn't been easy – but I guess someone had to do it!

Apart from the obvious perks to the job I began to notice that I hadn't met a winemaker who didn't cook or who served bad coffee. Of course, winemakers are passionate and dedicated professionals, but what they really understand is how to indulge their senses. It was this realisation that inspired me to create *Dining With Wine*.

I asked thirty of Australia's leading winemakers to share their favourite recipe and tell me which wine they most enjoy with the meal. I then asked each of them to explain why they felt it was a perfect blend of flavours. The result, *Dining With Wine*, is a very personal insight into their thoughts.

What winemakers have taught me is that there are some basic principles to consider when matching food and wine – but that the real fun begins when you have the confidence to start experimenting.

What you are trying to achieve is a balance. The combination of flavours should compliment each other. A dish with delicate flavours should be matched to a delicate wine. John Edwards pairs his Gathering Sauvignon Blanc with oyster shooters (page 11). With this match the subtle flavour of the oysters is not to be overpowered. A more intense dish can be matched with a more hearty wine. Ben Glaetzer pairs his robust Heartland Shiraz with the rich flavours of a beef cutlet, blue cheese butter and green beans (page 55).

You should also consider how well matched the flavours are. Pick out one or two dominant flavours in the dish and match these with similar flavours in the wine. Steve

Pannel identifies the nutty flavours in his recipe for pistachio pesto and matches it to the nutty and toasted bread characters of the Picardy Chardonnay (page 5). If in doubt about how to identify the flavours exhibited by a wine begin by reading the label – it's a really useful source of information!

Once you've begun to appreciate the interplay of flavours between the food and wine it's time to start having a bit of fun. Chester Osbourne, winemaker for d'Arenberg Wines, takes a different tack and disregards the old rule of white wine with white meat. Chester teams a chicken fillet stuffed with prosciutto and leek with his Custodian Grenache (page 31). Chester argues that the earthy and spicy character of the wine highlights the rustic nature of the dish.

All of the recipes in *Dining With Wine* are very tasty and straightforward enough to be prepared by anyone with the coordination to pull the cork on a bottle! The wine matches are, of course, perfect. Let's face it; even if you burn the food, you can still enjoy the wine!

Cheers!

Chris Jenkin
Producer, *Off the Vine*

For more information contact info@diningwithwine.net.au

Pistachio Pesto

Serve with Picardy Chardonnay

Ingredients

2 garlic cloves, peeled and crushed
20 mint leaves
pinch sea salt
200 g unsalted pistachios, shelled
6 tablespoons Parmesan, finely grated
freshly ground black pepper, to taste
300 ml extra virgin olive oil
800 g linguine or fettuccine
4 litres salted water

Method

Pesto: The pesto can be made in a mortar or a blender, although the mortar gives the best result. Place garlic, mint and salt in mortar and grind until smooth. If using salted pistachios do not include the pinch of salt. Add pistachios and continue to grind. Add Parmesan, pepper and oil and continue to grind until the mixture is well combined.

Pasta: Boil water and cook pasta until al dente. Drain and return to saucepan. Stir the pesto through the pasta.

Serve immediately with a sprinkling of grated Parmesan and a rocket salad.

"In this dish the most important characters are the nutty flavours of the pistachios and the rich texture of the olive oil. With this in mind I would choose a cool climate oak aged Chardonnay, such as Picardy. The nutty and toasted bread characters of the barrel fermentation and lees stirring match the pistachio flavours and the fresh acidity helps cut through and balance the olive oil."

Steve Pannell Winemaker and Consultant, Pannell Wine Consulting

Stuffed Zucchini Flowers

serves **4**

Serve with Henschke Tilly's Vineyard

Zucchinis and their delectable flowers are available all year round and are very easy to grow, particularly during the warmer months. Alternatively, the flowers can be ordered through your local grocer.

Ingredients

Flowers
2 tablespoons olive oil
3 tablespoons shallots, finely diced
1 tablespoon capers, chopped
zest of 1 lemon
1 tablespoon parsley, chopped
16 basil leaves
1 sprig of tarragon, chopped
200 g quark (or ricotta)
salt and freshly ground black pepper, to taste
16 zucchini flowers

Sauce
4 tablespoons olive oil
1 small onion, finely diced
2 garlic cloves, chopped
500 ml tomatoes, finely diced
3 tablespoons white wine

Method

Flowers: Gently heat oil in a small pan and brown shallots. Allow to cool. Combine capers, zest, parsley, basil, tarragon and quark/ricotta in a bowl and stir in cooled shallots. Season. Spoon or pipe this mixture into the zucchini flower cavities and fold the petals over the mixture. Place the flowers in a steamer and steam for 5 minutes.

Sauce: Gently heat oil in the pan and sauté onion until golden. Add garlic and sauté. Add tomato and wine. Bring to boil and remove from heat.

Serve the zucchini flowers on a bed of warm sauce and scatter with extra basil leaves.

"The crisp citrus and floral flavours of the Tilly's Vineyard are a good match for the zucchini flowers, offsetting the tangy citrus filling and the leafy acidic tomato sauce."

Stephen Henschke Winemaker, Henschke

Three Olive Putanesca

Serve with Bird in Hand Cabernet Sauvignon

Ingredients

olive oil
3 garlic cloves, chopped
2 fresh red chillies, diced
5–10 anchovy fillets, diced
1/3 cup Kalamata olives, pitted
1/3 cup Verdale olives, pitted
1/3 cup Manzanillo olives, pitted
2 tablespoons small capers
12 tomatoes, diced (800 g tin diced tomatoes)
pinch sea salt
4 litres salted water
800 g spaghetti
2 tablespoons fresh parsley, chopped
Parmesan cheese, grated

Method

Sauce: Heat oil in deep frying pan and fry garlic and chillies until the garlic browns. Add anchovies, olives and capers and stir. Add tomatoes and salt. Simmer, stirring intermittently, for 30 minutes to reduce into a thick sauce.

Spaghetti: Boil water and cook spaghetti until al dente. Drain and return to pot. Pour 3/4 of the sauce and 1/2 the parsley onto the spaghetti and combine until the spaghetti is well coated.

Serve in large bowls with a generous spoonful of the extra sauce, parsley and Parmesan on top.

"Bird in Hand Cabernet 2001 is incredibly soft and elegant. The wine's blackberry and chocolate palate perfectly compliments the intriguing spice and richness of this putanesca'."

Andrew Nugent Winemaker, Bird in Hand

Awesome Summer Starters

Serve with The Lane Gathering Sauvignon Semillon

Shooters

24 fresh oysters in the half shell
1 bottle The Lane Gathering Sauvignon
   Semillon
1 lime, juiced and zested

Slide a knife under the oyster to cut
through the muscle that attaches it to
the bottom shell. Leave the oyster resting
in the shell and pour a little Gathering
Sauvignon Semillon over the top. You can
add a squeeze of lime and zest if you like.
Tip the oyster into the mouth and chase
with a full glass of Gathering Sauvignon
Semillon. Smooth!

Red Baguettes

300 g roasted red peppers in oil
   (available from the deli section of most
   supermarkets)
olive oil
1 baguette with crunchy crust
300 g goat curd (cheese)
freshly ground white pepper, to taste

Drain oil from peppers and slice lengthwise
into 1 cm strips. Cut the baguette at an
angle into 1 cm thick slices. Spread a
liberal dob of goat curd on every slice.
Curl the red pepper strips on top and finish
with a dash of oil and a grind of white
pepper. Luscious!

"This wine has the structure and finesse of Europe's best.
Complemented by intense fine fruit flavours and spice, it's the
product of Australian sunlight and the terroir of The Lane. If
there's a better wine to enjoy with oysters, I haven't tasted it!"

John Edwards Vigneron, The Lane

Ingredients

Sauce
100 ml white wine
1¹/₂ tablespoons lemon juice
100 ml thickened cream
120 g chilled unsalted butter, cubed
¹/₂ tablespoon chives, chopped
salt and freshly ground white pepper, to taste

Salad
1 medium fennel bulb, thinly sliced
3 witlof, thinly sliced
1 small red onion, diced
1 punnet cherry tomatoes, halved
2 tablespoons lemon juice
2 tablespoons extra virgin olive oil

Garfish
8 medium garfish fillets, butterflied
16 sage leaves
8 prosciutto slices
2 tablespoons olive oil

Method

Sauce: Combine Semillon and lemon juice in small saucepan. Reduce by half over a medium heat. Add cream, stir and reduce by half over medium heat. Add chilled butter and whisk until combined. Remove from heat. Add chives and season to taste. Keep warm.

Salad: Combine salad ingredients in bowl. Toss and season to taste.

Garfish: Lay fish fillets skin side down. Place two sage leaves on top and cover with a slice of prosciutto. Heat oil in a non-stick frying pan. Fry each fillet, skin side down for 1 minute. Transfer the fillets to a baking dish with the prosciutto side facing up and grill under a griller for 2 minutes.

Pour sauce over garfish and serve with the salad.

"The Goss Corner vineyard was only planted to Semillon vines in 1996 yet this third vintage shows superb characteristics of the variety. Delicate whiffs of fresh meadow hay, a citrus nose which goes right through to the palate and wonderful acidity means the Goss Corner is perfect with the delicate white soft flesh of the garfish, complimenting, rather than overwhelming it."

Ben Riggs Winemaker, Penny's Hill

Saltimbocca
of Garfish

serves **4**

Serve with Penny's Hill Goss Corner Semillon

Steamed Atlantic Salmon
with Asparagus and Salmon Roe

serves **4**

Serve with Penfolds Thomas Hyland Chardonnay

Ingredients

4 Atlantic salmon portions (600 g), skin on
1 tablespoon olive oil
4 bunches thin green asparagus (about
  10 per bunch)
100 ml fish stock
1 tablespoon white wine
2 tablespoons cream
100 g unsalted butter, melted
sea salt and freshly ground white pepper,
  to taste
20 g salmon roe
1/2 bunch chives, chopped

Method

Sauce: Place stock and wine in a saucepan over medium heat. Stir and reduce by one third. Add cream, stir and bring to the boil. Remove from heat. Add butter and whisk until the sauce is thick and smooth. Place the salmon roe and chives into the warm sauce. Season, stir and keep warm.

Salmon: Brush salmon all over with olive oil, place in steamer and steam for up to 4 minutes. It is cooked when you press the top of the salmon and feel it give way under your fingertips.

Asparagus: Cut 2cm off asparagus stems. Drop the spears into lightly salted boiling water for 30 seconds. Remove and refresh in cold water. Drain and pour melted butter over asparagus. Season.

Arrange the salmon and asparagus on warmed serving plates. Top with the sauce and garnish with extra salmon roe.

"An elegant and restrained Chardonnay is the perfect accompaniment to a grilled salmon steak. The zesty lemon finish of the Thomas Hyland Chardonnay is the perfect way to cut through the creaminess of the sauce with the salmon."

Oliver Crawford Winemaker, Penfolds

Oven baked Flathead

Serve with Devil's Lair Margaret River Chardonnay

Ingredients

10 kipfler potatoes, peeled and diced
50 g unsalted butter
8 sage leaves, finely chopped
2 tablespoons balsamic vinegar
2 flathead fillets, trimmed
sea salt and freshly ground black pepper, to taste
2 tablespoons olive oil
4 shallots, peeled and trimmed

Method

Heat oven to 220°C (450°F). Boil the potatoes in salted water until tender. Drain, cover with the lid and set aside. Place butter, sage and vinegar in a small pan and heat over a low heat for 5 minutes. Place fish and shallots in an oven dish. Season and drizzle with oil. Cook in oven for 15 minutes. Remove from the oven. Arrange the potatoes on warmed plates and top with the fish, shallots and butter sauce.

"The complex amalgam of roasted cashews, pear essence and pink grapefruit overlaid with subtle oak from the Devil's Lair Chardonnay compliment the flathead and its fresh herbs and butter."

Stuart Pym Winemaker, Devil's Lair

Pemberton Yabbies

serves 4

Serve with Houghton Pemberton Chardonnay

Ingredients

800 g fresh fettuccini
4 litres salted water
1 tablespoon olive oil
1 garlic clove, chopped
1 onion, diced
16 raw yabbies, shelled
400 g tin crushed tomatoes
$\frac{1}{3}$ cup white wine
150 ml cream
100 g walnuts, crushed
sea salt and freshly ground black pepper,
  to taste

Method

Boil water and cook fettuccini until al dente. Drain, cover and set aside. Heat oil in a pan and cook the garlic, onion and yabbies for 5 minutes. Add tomatoes and wine and stir over a low heat until reduced by half. Add cream, stir and season. Add the fettuccini and combine.

Serve with cracked walnuts sprinkled over the top.

"I love eating yabbies and for that reason I always make sure the damn at Pemberton is well stocked with them. Summer isn't the same without them. This yabbie dish works brilliantly with the Pemberton Chardonnay. The wine's tight fine acid cuts through the oil of the yabbie and contributes its own depth and texture."

Simon Osicka   Winemaker, Houghton Wines

Ingredients

350 g plain flour, sifted
1 teaspoon baking powder
1 teaspoon paprika
salt and freshly ground black pepper,
   to taste
5 eggs
250 ml milk
200 ml olive oil
2 teaspoons garlic, crushed
600 g grated pumpkin
120 g basil, chopped
120 g chives, chopped
120 g coriander, chopped
200 ml vegetable oil
16 king prawns, shelled and deveined
   with tails intact
220 g crème fraiche

Method

Fritters: combine flour, baking powder, paprika and seasoning in a bowl. In a separate bowl whisk eggs, milk, oil and garlic. Gradually pour wet mixture on to flour mixture and stir. When mixture is smooth, add grated pumpkin and herbs. Heat 1 tablespoon of vegetable oil in a non-stick fry pan. Drop 1 tablespoon of batter per fritter in pan. Cook 2 fritters at a time. Cook on each side until golden brown. Batter should yield 16 fritters. Before serving, trim edges with knife or cookie cutter and keep warm.

Prawns: Steam prawns over boiling water for 8 minutes.

Arrange 4 prawns with 4 fritters per plate with a dollop of crème fraiche and a sprinkle of paprika on fritters and serve with a green salad.

"Viognier is a very versatile wine when it comes to food matching as it is fragrant and intense while at the same time rich, opulent and low in natural acidity. It complements a wide range of foods as the many flavours and facets of the wine come out in different circumstances."

Louisa Rose
Louisa Rose Winemaker, Yalumba

www.yalumba.com

Steamed Prawns
and Pumpkin Fritters

serves **4**

Serve with Yalumba Viognier

Ingredients

Marinade
$1/_4$ cup lime juice
$1/_2$ cup rice vinegar
$1/_2$ cup castor sugar
1 red chilli
pinch salt

Salad
350 g green papaya, grated
24 medium prawns, cooked
1 mango, finely sliced
$1/_2$ cup mint
$1/_2$ cup basil
$1/_2$ cup Vietnamese hot mint (raw ram)
$1/_2$ cup unsalted peanuts, shelled and
  crushed
$1/_2$ cup shallots, finely sliced
extra mint, basil and Vietnamese hot mint
  to serve

Dipping sauce
$1/_3$ cup castor sugar
$1/_3$ cup fresh lime juice
$1/_3$ cup fish sauce (nuoc nam)
1 garlic clove, crushed
1 small red chilli, finely chopped

Method

Marinade: Combine ingredients in a medium bowl. Add the green papaya and marinate for a maximum of 30 minutes.

Dipping sauce: Add sugar to lime juice and stir to dissolve the sugar. Add fish sauce, garlic and chilli and stir well.

Salad: Drain the marinated papaya and combine it with the prawns, mango, mint, basil and hot mint and $1/_4$ cup of the dipping sauce. Transfer the salad to serving plates and sprinkle with peanuts, shallots and the extra mint, basil and hot mint.

Serve with the remaining fish dipping sauce.

"Warm days and the best of fresh seafood and tropical fruits provide the perfect recipe for enjoying a glass or two of Bin 7. It will pick you up with its zesty freshness, and deliver a long, persistent finish. Enjoy."

Kerri Thompson Winemaker,
Leasingham Wines

Chilli Crabs

 serves 4

Serve with Chapel Hill Verdelho

Ingredients

2 tablespoons peanut oil
2 tablespoons fresh ginger, finely grated
3 garlic cloves, finely chopped
2 tablespoons sweet chilli sauce
$1/3$ cup chilli sauce
1 tablespoon light soy sauce
$1/3$ cup tomato sauce
1 tablespoon sugar
300 ml water
3 kg raw blue swimmer crabs
1 cup peanut oil

"This is messy, absolutely delicious finger food. I love the performance of claw picks and crackers, bibs and finger bowls. Old white wines cry out to be challenged by something as flavourful as chilli crabs"

P. A Dunsford.

Pam Dunsford
Winemaker, Chapel Hill

Method

Sauce: Heat 2 tablespoons of oil in a saucepan and fry ginger and garlic until cooked but not brown. Add the sweet chilli, chilli, soy and tomato sauces and sugar and bring to boil. Add water and simmer uncovered for 25 minutes, reducing the sauce by half.

Crabs: To open the crabs lift up the abdominal flap (small triangle on the crab's underside), slip your thumb under the shell and prise the top shell off. Remove the gills and intestines under cool running water. Cut the crabs in half (or quarters if they are larger). Heat $1/2$ cup of oil in a wok or large saucepan until it is very hot. Fry half the crab pieces until they turn pink. Using a fine sieve remove any burnt material from the oil. Add another $1/2$ cup of oil, heat to very hot and cook the remaining crabs. Drain on absorbent paper.

Coat the crabs in the sauce and serve with sprigs of coriander and jasmine rice.

Green Point Seafood Soup

serves 6

Serve with Green Point Pinot Noir

"The Green Point Pinot Noir has a wonderfully complex array of dark cherry, spice and bramble characters, with a beautifully balanced, silky texture. This wine works really well with the rich seafood flavours and spice of the soup. A food and wine match to warm your heart. Enjoy!"

James Gosper Winemaker, Domaine Chandon

Ingredients

Stock

20 medium uncooked prawns
4 uncooked blue swimmer crabs
150 ml olive oil
2 tablespoons butter
2 carrots, diced
1 onion, diced
1/2 bunch of celery, diced
4 cloves of garlic, crushed
1/2 bunch parsley
2 small red chillies, sliced
300 g fish bones
75 ml white wine
30 ml white wine vinegar
400 g tinned tomatoes
4 litres chicken stock
muslin (or very fine sieve)

Soup

8 shallots, peeled and diced
sea salt to taste
2 tablespoons tomato paste
Tabasco sauce, to taste
2 white fish fillets (eg flathead), cubed
2 oily fish fillets (eg tuna), cubed
20 uncooked mussels
15 uncooked scallops
small bunch baby spinach

Method

Stock: Shell the prawns and crabs. Put meat aside. Smash crab shells into small pieces and fry with the prawn shells in a little oil until they turn pink. Put cooked shells aside. Heat oil and butter in a large pot. Add carrots, onion, celery, garlic, parsley and chillies. Fry until soft. Add fish bones, wine and vinegar and cook for 4 minutes. Add the fried shells, tomatoes and stock. Cook on low heat for 2 hours. Regularly skim the fat and froth from the surface so that it remains clear. Allow to cool in the pot. Once cool skim the top and strain through the muslin. Set aside.

Soup: Reheat the fish stock and add shallots, salt, tomato paste and Tabasco. Add all the uncooked seafood ingredients and simmer for 5 minutes until the seafood is opaque. Remove any unopened mussels. Add the spinach and stir.

Serve with warm crusty bread rubbed with butter and garlic.

Ingredients

Stuffing
400 g chicken thighs, skinned and cubed
sea salt and freshly ground black pepper,
   to taste
2 teaspoons fresh thyme
1 teaspoon dried boletus mushrooms
200 ml white wine
2 tablespoons olive oil
2 tablespoons of butter
200 g prosciutto, finely diced
100 g leeks, finely diced
2 egg whites
400 ml cream

Chicken
4 large chicken breasts
2 tablespoons olive oil

Beans
400 g tin canelli beans

1 teaspoon truffle oil
(optional)

Glaze
3 litres chicken stock
1 litre beef stock
1 garlic clove, peeled

Method

Pre-heat the oven to 180ºC (350º).

Stuffing: Season chicken cubes and combine with thyme, mushrooms and wine. Cover and refrigerate for 1 hour. Heat oil and butter in a pan and gently fry prosciutto and leeks to soften. Set aside to cool. Process the refrigerated mixture in food processor until it is a fine mince. Scrape down the sides and add egg whites. Continue to process slowly adding the cream. Stir in prosciutto and leeks and season to taste.

Chicken: Make an incision at the thicker end of the fillets and drive the knife inside the fillet creating a pocket. Use a small spoon to fill the pocket with the stuffing. Heat oil in pan and seal both sides of the stuffed fillets. Transfer to an ovenproof dish and cook in the oven for up to 10 minutes. Allow to rest for 5 minutes before carving.

Beans: Drain beans, puree in blender, heat in microwave and stir in truffle oil

Glaze: Pour stock into pan and add garlic. Bring to boil. Simmer, skimming stock regularly, until reduced by $3/4$. Remove garlic.

Arrange the chicken on the beans, drizzle with the glaze and garnish with extra grilled prosciutto.

Chicken with Prosciutto
and Leek Stuffing

serves **4**

Serve with d'Arenberg The Custodian Grenache

"Here is the perfect example of a reversal to the proverb of whites with white and reds with red. For this chicken dish, The Custodian's balance of fruity intensity and fine integrated tannins stand up beautifully to the ethereal base notes of truffles and the salty sweetness of the prosciutto and leek stuffing. The earthy and spicy character of the wine highlights the rustic texture of the white bean puree and the velvety stickiness of the glaze."

Chester Osbourne Chief Winemaker & Viticulturist, d'Arenberg

Chicken Casserole

Serve with Jacob's Creek Reserve Chardonnay

Ingredients

1¹/₂ tablespoons olive oil
2 kg chicken pieces
225 g baby onions, peeled
150 g pancetta, diced
225 g Swiss brown or open field
  mushrooms, thick slices
8 sprigs fresh thyme, leaves removed
3 cups white wine
1 cup chicken stock
2 tablespoons butter
2 tablespoons plain flour
1 bay leaf
2 tablespoons parsley, finely chopped

Method

Preheat oven to 170°C.

Heat olive oil in a heavy based pan, brown chicken all over. Transfer to a casserole dish and season.

In same pan brown onions, pancetta, mushrooms and thyme. Remove to casserole dish. Pour wine into pan and boil for 1 minute. Add stock. Combine butter and flour to create a paste. Stir paste into sauce to thicken sauce. Pour the sauce into casserole dish; add bay leaf and sprinkle with parsley. Cover with lid and cook in oven for 1 hour.

Serve with celeriac and parsnip mash.

"The peach and melon flavours of the Jacob's Creek Reserve Chardonnay complement the warm flavours of the dish and the citrus palate provides a nice foil to the richness of the cooking. All in all an elegant dish with an elegant wine."

Philip Lafer   Winemaker, Jacob's Creek

Ingredients

Aioli
2 egg yolks
$1/2$ tablespoon apple cider vinegar
$1/2$ teaspoon Dijon mustard
1 garlic clove, crushed
500 ml vegetable oil
1 preserved lemon, rind finely sliced
sea salt and freshly ground black pepper,
   to taste

Spatchcocks
4 spatchcocks (size 4), trimmed
500 ml soy sauce
$1^1/2$ litres water
4 whole garlic bulbs, roughly chopped
100 g whole ginger root, roughly chopped
4 star-anise pods

Method

Aioli: For best results prepare the aioli the day prior. Process yolks, vinegar, mustard and garlic in blender. Blend and slowly add oil until mixture gradually thickens. Season and stir in preserved lemon rind.

Spatchcocks: Preheat oven to 150°C (300°F). Place spatchcocks in a deep oven dish. Combine soy and water and pour over spatchcocks, ensuring they are fully submerged. Add remaining ingredients to the liquid. Cover tightly with foil and place in oven for 50 minutes. Remove from oven and allow to cool in the liquid. For best results, refrigerate overnight in liquid to infuse flavours and colour. Preheat oven to 180°C (350°F). Drain spatchcocks, place in roasting dish and cook uncovered in oven for up to 20 minutes until golden in colour.

Serve with aioli and a rocket salad.

"This Asian-inspired recipe incorporates some very robust flavours which are well complemented by the full-bodied, and rich, spicy fruit characters of this great McLaren Vale Shiraz – The Vincent".

Jon Ketley Winemaker, Tapestry

www.tapestrywines.com.au

Twice Cooked Spatchcock
with Preserved Lemon Aioli

serves **4**

Serve with Tapestry The Vincent Shiraz

Balsamic Chicken Liver Paté

serves 6

Serve with Coldstream Hills Pinot Noir

Ingredients

Caramelised Balsamic
500 ml balsamic vinegar
250 g castor sugar

Paté
1 kg unsalted butter
3 onions, finely diced
1 tablespoon garlic, crushed
1 kg chicken liver, cleaned and soaked
   overnight in milk
1 teaspoon cloves, finely ground
500 ml thickened cream
8 large eggs
salt and freshly ground black pepper,
   to taste

Jelly
280 ml chicken stock
7 g unflavoured gelatine
red peppercorns and fresh thyme to
   decorate

**"The Pinot Noir is a medium bodied
wine with attractive plum, cherry and
gamey fruit characters. The tannin
structure is fine and persistent providing
both texture and structure to the wine
and complimenting the paté beautifully."**

Andrew Fleming Winemaker, Coldstream Hills

Method

Caramelised Balsamic: Combine vinegar
and castor sugar in a saucepan. Bring to
the boil while stirring. Allow to simmer and
reduce by half. Allow to cool.

Paté: Preheat oven to 160°C (325°F). Heat
butter in a pan and sauté onions and garlic
until brown. Allow to cool. Place in a blender
along with livers, cloves, cream, eggs and
the caramelised balsamic mixture. Blend
until reaches a smooth paste. Strain through
a fine sieve and pour into 6 ramekins. Place
ramekins on a deep oven tray and pour
water into the tray until it reaches half way
up the ramekin sides. Cook for 15 to 20
minutes (or until paté is set). Cool.

Jelly: Dissolve the gelatine in the stock by
following the directions on the gelatine
packet. Carefully put the jelly bowl into a
bowl of ice water and stir until it
is less than room temperature.
Ensure iced water does not
get into the jelly bowl. Pour
jelly mixture over paté and
decorate with peppercorns
and thyme. Refrigerate to set.

Serve at room temperature
with toasted brioche,
sea salted butter and
cornichons.

Ingredients

4 large duck breasts
sea salt and freshly ground black pepper,
  to taste
1 teaspoon of cayenne pepper
olive oil
200 ml chicken stock
4 tablespoons honey
4 tablespoons soy sauce
2 tablespoons fresh ginger, grated
2 small fresh red chillies, sliced
4 tablespoons rice wine or dry sherry
squeeze of lime juice
2 teaspoons cornflour

"This full flavoured dish calls for a
wine of great balance.
Our Epiphany brims with
rich dark berry aromas
supported by subtle oak,
which moulds snugly
around the ginger, soy and
lime. A perfect match to
a fabulous meal."

Stuart Bourne
Winemaker, Barossa Valley Estate

Method

Preheat oven to 200°C. Warm a shallow
oven dish in the oven.

Duck: Trim excess fat from duck breasts and
score the skin side with a sharp knife. Rub
the skin with salt and season the rest of the
breast with salt, pepper and cayenne. Heat
oil in a heavy pan. Cook the breasts skin
side down for 5 minutes over a low heat.
The skin should become brown and crisp.
Remove and discard excess fat from the pan,
turn breasts over and cook for 1 minute to
seal other side. Transfer breasts to oven
dish and place into oven for 10 minutes.
Remove from oven, cover dish with foil
and allow to rest in a warm place whilst
preparing the sauce.

Sauce: Pour stock, honey, soy, ginger, chilli,
rice wine and lime into original pan. Then
take 4 tablespoons of liquid from pan and
put in a small bowl. Add cornflour to it, stir
and dissolve. Return it to the pan, bring to
boil and stir gently for 2 minutes.

Thinly slice breasts, arrange on warm plates
and pour over a little sauce. Serve with
sesame and soba noodle salad.

Roast Duck
with Zingy Ginger Sauce

serves 4

Serve with Barossa Valley Estate Epiphany Shiraz

Duck Risotto

serves 4

Serve with Rosemount Estate Grenache Syrah Mourvedre

Ingredients

1 BBQ duck (available from Chinese Butcher or Restaurant)
3 litres water
olive oil
200 g Shitake mushrooms, finely diced
3 stalks spring onion, finely chopped
2 cloves garlic, finely chopped
$1/2$ cup parsley, chopped
1 kg Arborio rice
1 tablespoon oyster sauce
1 tablespoon hoisin sauce

"The Grenach Syrah Mourvedre, or GSM, is one of the wines in the Rosemount Estate Epicurean Collection. We blended this collection of wines with the intention that they should be enjoyed with food. We created wines with layers of flavour and we hope you will discover why the GSM is the ideal match for the multiple flavours of this delicious duck risotto."

Charles Wish

Charles Wish – Winemaker, Rosemount Estate

Method

Stock: Remove all meat and skin from the duck. Dice and set it aside for the risotto. Bring water to boil in a large pot and add duck bones. Simmer until water is reduced by 75%. Strain through a fine sieve into a medium saucepan and keep warm on a low heat. Discard the sieve contents.

Risotto: Heat oil in a pan and fry mushrooms, spring onion, garlic and parsley for 2 minutes. Add the diced meat and skin to the pan and cook for 2 minutes. Set aside. Heat oil in medium pan over medium heat and add rice. Stir rice for 3 minutes ensuring it is thoroughly coated in oil. Add one cup of warm duck stock and stir until it is almost completely absorbed by the rice. Repeat this process until the rice is firm but cooked. The rice should not become dry at any stage through this process but remain wet and thick. Add oyster and hoisin sauces and stir. Fold the pan-fried ingredients through the rice, season and serve in warmed bowls.

GSM

GRENACHE SYRAH MOURVEDRE
McLAREN VALE · BAROSSA VALLEY
LANGHORNE CREEK

ROSEMOUNT

Cassoulet

Serve with Penfolds Thomas Hyland Shiraz

Ingredients

3 tablespoons olive oil
4 Italian sausages, sliced
150 g bacon, diced
500 g boneless pork shoulder, diced
4 duck legs
250 g tin white beans
4 garlic cloves, crushed
1 large onion, chopped
2 carrots, cubed
400 g tin chopped tomatoes
$1/2$ teaspoon dried thyme
2 bay leaves
1 litre chicken stock
sea salt and freshly ground black pepper,
to taste
1 cup breadcrumbs
2 tablespoons parsley,
chopped

Method

Preheat oven to 160°C (325°F).

Heat olive oil in a heavy saucepan and sauté the sausage, bacon, pork and duck until browned. Place the meat, beans, garlic, onion, carrots, tomatoes, thyme and bay leaves in a heavy oven dish. Add stock to cover by 5cm. Cover with a lid. Place in oven and cook for up to 3 hours. Remove from the oven. Season. Scatter the breadcrumbs and parsley over the top and place under a hot grill until the breadcrumbs brown.

Serve with chunks of crusty white bread.

"Cassoulet is the perfect dish for a dinner with good friends, great wine and animated conversation. I can prepare it ahead of time and then sit back and enjoy the company and the wines with my guests. I love to serve it in an authentic European way with hunks of crusty bread, lashings of wine and political debate."

Peter Gago   Winemaker, Penfolds

Rolled Loin of Pork

serves 4

Serve with Stephen John Traugott Cuvee Sparkling Shiraz Pinot Noir

Ingredients

1 cup prunes, pitted
1 cup port wine
2 kg boned loin of pork
$1/2$ cup almonds, slivered
olive oil
salt
butcher's twine

"This recipe was handed down from my grandmother. She always served it cold at special occasion family luncheons. The flavours can be manipulated by using different wines for marinating the prunes. You could try Muscat, Amontillado Sherry or Vintage Port. It is best to use a high quality aged fortified wine, as the aged fruit and rancio characters are infused into the meat during cooking."

Stephen John Winemaker, Stephen John Wines

Method

Soak prunes in port overnight.

Preheat over to 230°C (475°F).

Lay the pork loin out flat. Lay prunes and almonds evenly across the loin. Roll up loin and tie tightly with butcher's twine. Score the outside of the rind at 1 cm intervals. Rub all over with olive oil and salt. Place pork loin on a rack in a baking dish and bake uncovered in oven for $1/2$ hour. Reduce heat to 180°C (350°F) and bake for a further $1^1/2$ hours or until cooked through. The rind should be crisp and crackling.

This recipe can be served hot with steamed beans, roast potatoes and gravy made from the pan juices.

If serving it cold, allow the roast to cool and refrigerate overnight. Next day carve into slices (including crackling) and place on a large serving platter. Serve with creamy cucumber salad.

Moroccan Lamb
and Pear Tagine
 serves 4

Serve with Wynns Coonawarra Estate Cabernet Sauvignon

Ingredients

olive oil
1 kg lean lamb, cut into 4cm cubes
2 large onions, peeled & sliced
1 teaspoon cumin
1 teaspoon ground coriander
1 teaspoon ground ginger
1 teaspoon cinnamon
1 teaspoon black pepper
1 cup of water
salt, to taste
4 firm pears, peeled, cored & cut into
    4 cm chunks
1/2 cup sultanas
1/2 cup slivered almonds
4 tablespoons veal glace (optional)

Method

Heat olive oil in large saucepan and brown the lamb. Remove from pan and set aside. Drain the pan; add more oil and fry onion until soft. Add lamb back to the pan along with cumin, coriander, ginger, cinnamon and pepper. Stir well then add water and season with salt.

Cover with a lid and simmer for up to 2 hours until the meat is tender.

Add the pears, sultanas, almonds and veal glace (for a thicker and richer sauce) to the saucepan and cook for a further 5 minutes until the pears are just soft.

Serve with saffron couscous.

"Our Cabernet Sauvignon is a full-bodied wine with characteristic strong mint and berry flavours. It has fine structure and a depth of flavour which perfectly compliments the layers of flavour in the Moroccan Lamb & Pear Tagine. What a partnership!"

Sue Hodder

Sue Hodder Winemaker, Wynns Coonawarra Estate

44

Roast Lamb
with Baked Vegetables

serves 4

Serve with Pauletts Polish Hill River Cabernet Merlot

Ingredients

Baste
$1/2$ cup red wine
$1/4$ cup balsamic vinegar
$1/4$ cup olive oil

Roast
2 kg leg of lamb
1 tablespoon sea salt
1 tablespoon lemon pepper
$1/4$ cup oil
2 garlic cloves, crushed
freshly ground black pepper, to taste
400 g pumpkin, thickly sliced
400 g potato, thickly sliced
400 g parsnip, thickly sliced
400 g carrot, thickly sliced

Gravy
1 cup red wine
$1/2$ cup balsamic vinegar
$1/2$ cup water
2 tablespoons brown sugar

"I highly recommend using Saltbush Lamb for this recipe if your butcher can source it. The depth of flavours of the lamb harmonise very well with the savouriness, rich berry flavours and firm tannins of the Cabernet Sauvignon and Merlot grapes."

Neil Paulett

Neil Paulett Winemaker, Paulett Wines

Method

Baste: Combine ingredients in a small bowl.

Roast: Preheat oven to 220°C. Rub lamb all over with sea salt and lemon pepper. Place in an oiled oven dish and cook in the oven for $1/2$ hour. Reduce oven temperature to 180°C. Spoon 2 tablespoons of baste over lamb. Continue to cook for up to 2 hours, basting every half hour. Combine oil, garlic and pepper and coat potato, pumpkin, parsnip and carrot. Place on an oven tray and cook for up to 45 minutes with the lamb. When cooked place on a warm serving platter and cover with foil to rest.

Gravy: Prepare gravy in same baking dish used to cook the lamb. Add wine, balsamic vinegar, water and sugar. Stir over a low heat scraping up all the "meat pieces" until reduced to a thick sauce.

Carve the lamb and serve with a generous spoonful of gravy alongside the roast vegetables and green peas.

47

Lamb Shanks

Serve with Seppelt Chalambar Shiraz

Ingredients

8 Frenched lamb shanks (butcher trims
   bone ends)
50 g flour
100 g olive oil
$^1/_2$ teaspoon rosemary
$^1/_2$ teaspoon coriander seeds, crushed
$^1/_2$ teaspoon dried chilli
$^1/_2$ teaspoon paprika
2 garlic cloves, crushed
1 carrot, diced
2 sticks celery, diced
2 onions, sliced
2 tablespoons red wine vinegar
$^3/_4$ cup red wine
1 cup beef stock
800 g tin crushed tomatoes

Method

Coat lamb in flour. Heat oil in a heavy pan
and quickly seal all sides of the lamb.
Add the rosemary, coriander seeds, chilli,
paprika, garlic, carrot, celery and onions.
Stir to cover the meat and vegetables in
the spices. Add the vinegar and wine and
simmer until it has reduced by half. Add
stock and tomatoes. Cover with a lid and
simmer over a low heat for 2 hours.

Serve with mashed potato and steamed
spinach

"Lamb slowly cooked in red wine and stock deserves a fuller-
bodied Shiraz which has a range of flavours, such as Seppelt
Chalambar."

Arthur O'Connor Winemaker, Seppelt

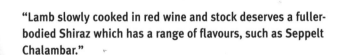

Lamb Racks with Dukkah Crust
and Yoghurt Mint Sauce

Serve with Scarpantoni School Block Shiraz Cabernet Merlot

Ingredients

Lamb Racks
3 slices of toasted bread
4 tablespoons dukkah
2 cloves garlic, crushed
2 tablespoons parsley, chopped
Rind of 1 lemon, finely grated
$1/4$ cup olive oil
salt and freshly ground black pepper, to taste
2 racks of 8 French trimmed lamb
2 tablespoons honey

Yoghurt Sauce
400 g natural yoghurt
1 garlic clove, crushed
4 tablespoons mint, finely chopped
1 lemon, juiced
salt and pepper, to taste

"School Block provides loads of spicy,
rich Shiraz to compliment the tender
lamb and dukkah crust. While the
varietal minty flavours of Cabernet
Sauvignon pay homage to the zesty
yoghurt accompaniment!"

Michael Scarpantoni Winemaker, Scarpantoni Estate Wines

Method

Lamb Racks: Preheat oven to 180°C (350°F).
Process toasted bread in blender until
breadcrumbs form. Place the breadcrumbs
in a bowl and combine with dukkah, garlic,
parsley, lemon rind, olive oil, salt and
pepper. Add a little more olive oil if it
looks too dry. Brush olive oil over lamb
racks and season. Heat frying pan and
place lamb fat side down in pan and sear
for 2 minutes. Remove and place on baking
tray. Brush top of lamb racks with honey
and press dukkah crumb mixture on top.
Bake in oven for up to 30 minutes. Remove
from oven, cover in foil and rest lamb for
5 minutes.

Yoghurt Sauce: Combine
and mix all the yoghurt
ingredients in a bowl and
set aside.

Cut lamb racks in half and
serve with broccolini and
the yoghurt sauce.

Braised Beef

Serve with 1998 Seppelt Vintage Fortified

Ingredients

1 kg blade steak, diced
4 bacon rashers, cut into 2cm pieces
2 tablespoons olive oil
12 garlic cloves, peeled & whole
4 onions, diced
4 sticks celery, diced
2 large carrots, diced
2 red capsicum, diced
4 egg tomatoes, diced
1 tablespoon plain flour
1 cup red wine
1 teaspoon fresh thyme
1 litre beef stock
salt and freshly ground black pepper,
  to taste

Method

Preheat oven to 150°C.

Heat oil in a heavy pan and brown diced beef and bacon. Remove from pan and set aside. Sauté garlic, onion, celery, carrot, capsicum and tomatoes in pan until golden. Sprinkle with flour and stir well. Add wine, stock and thyme. Simmer over a low heat until it begins to thicken. Add beef and bacon back to the pan and season. Transfer to oven dish and cook in oven for up to 1^1/$_2$ hours.

Serve with potatoes mashed with cream and garlic and topped with basil pesto.

"A basic rule of wine and food matching is 'like flavours with like flavours'. Rich, full-bodied, fortified wines are perfect with a rich, full-bodied beef casserole."

James Godfrey Winemaker, Seppelt

www.seppelt.com.au

Beef Cutlet with Green Beans
and Olive Tapenade

Serve with Heartland Shiraz

Ingredients

400 g salted butter, room temperature
200 g gorgonzola cheese, room
  temperature
80 g chives, finely sliced
4 beef cutlets
100 ml olive oil
salt and freshly ground black pepper,
  to taste
550 g green beans, finely sliced and
  blanched
250 g olive tapenade (paste)

"Vintage is over and there are no excuses left – it's time to start pulling my weight in the kitchen again! This dish is a winner. The ingredients are simple but they combine to make a hearty, richly flavoured meal. Our Heartland Shiraz from the Limestone Coast is a brilliant partner for this dish. The wine is big, vibrant and spicy. They're a great pair!"

Ben Glaetzer Winemaker, Heartland Wines

Method

Blue Cheese Butter: Place butter, gorgonzola and chives in a bowl and whisk until combined. Place mixture on grease-proof paper and roll into a cylinder. Wrap in foil and chill in refrigerator for at least 3 hours.

Beef: Preheat oven to 180°C (350°F). Rub cutlets with oil and season. Place cutlets in a very hot griddle pan and seal both sides. Remove cutlets and arrange in a roasting dish. Place in oven for up to 12 minutes. Remove beef from oven and allow to rest for 5 minutes prior to serving.

Beans: Immerse beans in boiling water for 3 minutes. Drain and combine well with the olive tapenade.

Serve on large plates with the beans in centre and the cutlet arranged on top, crowned with a disc of blue cheese butter.

Kangaroo
with Plum Sauce

serves 4

Serve with Nepenthe Pinot Noir

Ingredients

800 g kangaroo fillet
200 ml honey
200 ml beer
400 g plums, pitted
200 g sugar
400 ml water
6 tablespoons macadamia nut or olive oil
1 onion, diced
2 teaspoons garlic, crushed
2 red chillies, sliced
2 teaspoons brown sugar
extra macadamia nut or olive oil
salt and freshly ground black pepper, to taste
2 bunches bok choy
1 lime, juiced

Method

Fillet: Slice fillet into thin strips and place in a bowl. Add honey and beer. Cover and refrigerate for at least two hours. Brush a very hot chargrill with oil. Add kangaroo strips and cook for one minute on each side. Season.

Sauce: Place plums, sugar and water in a pan and bring to boil. Simmer for 20 minutes. Allow to cool and puree in a blender. Heat oil in a pan and sauté diced onion, garlic and chilli until onion is transparent. Add brown sugar and plum puree to the pan and simmer until begins to thicken.

Bok Choy: Blanche in boiling water. Remove and drain. Toss in a bowl with pepper, extra oil and lime juice.

Coat the kangaroo fillet in the sauce and serve with bok choy and lime wedges.

"I find that the bigger, fuller bodied wines such as Shiraz tend to overpower lighter Asian inspired dishes. I personally would always choose a Pinot style red wine to have with this type of food."

Peter Leske

Peter Leske Winemaker, Nepenthe

Botrytis Cake with Poached Pears
and Toffee Glaze

serves **10**

Serve with Woodstock Botrytis Sweet White

"Although Woodstock Botrytis Sweet White is lusciously sweet, the crisp, clean finish also ensures it matches many foods. The opulent apricot and mango flavours of the Botrytis blend well with the sweet poached pear, tangelo and cinnamon flavours absorbed into the cake and pears."

Scott Collett Winemaker, Woodstock Wine

Ingredients

Cake
8 egg whites
$1/_4$ teaspoon cream of tartar
$3/_4$ cup sugar
5 egg yolks
1 tablespoon tangelo or orange rind,
    finely grated
1 tablespoon almonds, ground
$1/_3$ cup olive oil
$1/_2$ cup Botrytis Sweet White
1 cup flour, sifted
pinch of salt

Pears
10 small pears with stems, peeled
    (beurre bosc)
500 ml white wine
500 ml Botrytis Sweet White
300 g sugar
pinch of saffron filaments
1 cinnamon stick
$1/_2$ tangelo or orange, sliced

Glaze
2 cups sugar
1 cup water
$1/_2$ tangelo or orange, finely sliced
1 cup poaching liquid (above)

Method

Cake: Preheat oven to 180°C (350°F).
Grease and line a 23 cm springform tin.
Beat egg whites, cream of tartar and
$1/_2$ cup of the sugar to a soft peak. Beat
yolks and remaining sugar until creamy.
Combine egg white and yolk mixtures and
fold in the remaining cake ingredients.
Bake in oven for 15 minutes. Reduce
temperature to 150°C and cook for 20
minutes. Cool on a wire rack.

Pears: Heat wines, sugar, saffron, cinnamon
and tangelo in pan over a low heat. Place
pears in pan and poach until tender.
Remove from heat. Retain liquid for glaze.

Glaze: Boil sugar, water and sliced tangelo
until a light brown colour. Immediately
remove from heat and carefully add 1 cup
of poaching liquid.

Dust cake with icing sugar
and cut into wedges. Place
a piece of cake on a plate
with a whole pear and drizzle
with the glaze. Serve with a
generous dollop of cream.

Ingredients

Syrup:
2 lemons, finely sliced
$^1/_2$ cup sugar
1 cup water

Custard:
4 eggs
$^3/_4$ cup sugar
3 lemons, juiced
$^3/_4$ cup cream

Toffee Crust:
1 litre water
500 g caster sugar

"The Sauvignon Blanc's ripe luscious fruit with a hint of sweetness and citrus is a perfect foil to the creamy richness of this refreshing dessert. Presenting a wonderful combination to enjoy at the end of a long, leisurely lunch, both can be easily transported to a favourite picnic spot or an al fresco setting in the garden."

David Fyffe
Winemaker, Yarra Burn

Method

Heat oven to 160°C (325°F).

Syrup: Place lemons, sugar and water in a saucepan and bring to boil. Simmer for up to 15 minutes reducing to syrup. Place 6 ramekins on an oven tray and divide syrup evenly between ramekins.

Custard: Blend eggs in a small bowl and strain through a coarse sieve into a larger bowl. Add sugar, lemon juice and cream. Mix thoroughly. Gently pour custard on top of lemon syrup in ramekins. Place tray in oven and bake for up to 20 minutes until custard has just set.

Toffee Crust: Boil water and sugar until the liquid colours to light amber. Remove from heat and pour onto baking tray. Allow to cool until hard. Break into pieces and place in a blender. Blend until resembles breadcrumbs. Sprinkle toffee crumbs on top of custard ramekins and place under a griller. Watch and remove as soon as the toffee melts. Remove from griller and allow to cool.

Serve at room temperature.

Lemon Syrup Brulee

serves 6

Serve with Yarra Burn Sauvignon Blanc Semillon

White Shiraz
& Lychee Sorbet

serves 4

Serve with Banrock Station White Shiraz

Ingredients

1 bottle Banrock Station White Shiraz
200 g icing sugar
420 g tin lychees

Method

Place Shiraz, icing sugar and lychees in a blender and blend until smooth.

Strain through a sieve into a tin tray with 3 cm sides.

Place the tray in the freezer.

As the sorbet begins to set rake it with a fork every 15 minutes to achieve nice fluffy flakes.

Serve in a shot glass as a palate cleanser between courses or serve a larger amount in a glass as a dessert.

"Salmon pink in colour, the Banrock Station White Shiraz displays fresh lifted strawberry flavours and a lovely fresh finish complimenting the sweetness of the lychees in this light dessert."

Paul Kassebaum Winemaker, Banrock Station

Published by East Street Publications
24 Park Terrace, Bowden, SA, 5007.
www.eaststreet.com.au

First published 2004

National Library of Australia
Cataloguing-in-Publication Entry
Dining With Wine: the perfect blend of food and wine from 30 of Australia's leading winemakers.
ISBN 0 9751145 5 7.
1. Cookery. 2. Wine and winemaking – Australia – Guidebooks. 3. Dinners and dining. I. Jenkin, Christopher James.
641.5

Cover Image: Beef Cutlet with Green Beans and Olive Tapanade served with Heartland Shiraz (page 54-55)

Back Cover Images: (from top) Kerri Thompson (Leasingham), Andrew Flemming (Coldstream Hills), Peter Gago (Penfolds), Ross Pament (Houghton), Andrew Nugent (Bird in Hand) and John Edwards (The Lane)

Styled by Todd Langley, The Works @ 18 Park
Photographed by Mike Annese, Blink
    Productions
Props generously provided by MYER
    (some stylists own)
Designed by Liz Nicholson, designBITE
Printed by Custom Press, 19 East Street,
    Brompton, SA, 5007